U.S. ARMY
GREEN BERET
MISSIONS

A TIMELINE

by Lisa M. Bolt Simons

CAPSTONE PRESS
a capstone imprint

Blazers Books are published by Capstone Press,
1710 Roe Crest Drive, North Mankato, Minnesota 56003
www.mycapstone.com

Library of Congress Cataloging-in-Publication Data
Simons, Lisa M. B., 1969– author.
U.S. Army Green Beret missions : a timeline / by Lisa M. Bolt Simons.
pages cm.—(Blazers. Special Ops mission timelines)
Includes bibliographical references and index.
Summary: "Introduces readers to major special operation missions of the US Special Forces Green Berets in a timeline format"—Provided by publisher.
Audience: Grade 4 to 6.
ISBN 978-1-4914-8702-0 (library binding)
ISBN 978-1-4914-8706-8 (eBook PDF)
1. United States. Army. Special Forces—Juvenile literature. I. Title. II. Title: United States Army Green Beret missions.
UA34.S64S54 2016
356′.167—dc23   2015026185

Editorial Credits
Aaron Sautter, editor; Kyle Grenz, designer; Jo Miller, media researcher;
Lori Barbeau, production specialist

Capstone Press would like to thank Michael Doidge, Military Historian, for his assistance in creating this book.

Photo Credits
Corbis, 9, Bettmann, 11, 15 (inset), Sygma/Patrick Chauvel, 5, 17; Getty Images: Hulton Archive/Keystone, 7, The LIFE Picture Collection/Larry Burrows, 13; Newscom/akg-images, 15, Dennis Brack, 19, European Press Agency/Anja_Niedringhaus, 23, Everett Collection, 21, KRT/David P. Gilkey, 25, Sipa USA/U.S. Army, 29, ZUMA Press/Timothy L. Hale, 4; Shutterstock/kanin.studio, Cover (silhouette); U.S. Air Force photo by Tech Sgt. Michael R. Holzworth, Cover (bottom inset); U.S. Army National Guard photo by Staff Sgt Shane Hamann, Cover (top inset); U.S. Army photo by Spc. Steven Young, 28, Staff Sgt. Brendan Stephens, 27

Design Elements
Getty Images: Photodisc; Shutterstock: ALMAGAMI

Printed in China by Nordica
1015/CA21501403
092015   009210S16

TABLE OF CONTENTS

Unconventional Soldiers

In World War II (1939–1945) the Office of Strategic Services (OSS) sent special teams to fight behind enemy lines. Their success led to the creation of the U.S. Army Special Forces in 1952. These **elite** soldiers have used **unconventional** warfare ever since.

elite—a group of people who have special advantages or talents

unconventional—a way of fighting that is not like ordinary hand-to-hand combat

Special Forces soldiers began wearing green berets in the 1950s. In 1961 president John F. Kennedy made the hats the official headgear of the U.S. Army Special Forces. These soldiers are now often known as the "Green Berets."

Operation Raincoat

December 3–9, 1943

In 1943 the 1st Special Service Force fought German troops on two mountains in Italy. The soldiers climbed a 200 foot (61 meter) cliff in the dark. They surprised the Germans and defeated them. Their success allowed the **Allies** to move freely through the Liri River valley.

Allies—a group of countries united against Germany during World War II, including France, the United States, Canada, Great Britain, and others

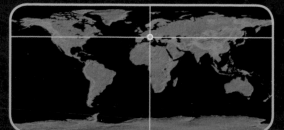

CONFLICT:
AT A GLANCE

Operation Raincoat

World War II

December 3-9, 1943

Location:
Liri River Valley, Italy

Mission goal:
help Allies travel through enemy territory

Mission outcome:
successful, but lost more than 75 percent of men

The 1st Special Service Force was activated on July 9, 1942. Its nickname was the "Devil's Brigade."

∧ The U.S. Army fired on a mountain to distract the Germans. Meanwhile, Special Service soldiers climbed up the cliffs behind the enemy.

1900   2000

Myitkyina Campaign

May 17, 1944

In 1944 Merrill's Marauders were sent to Burma. These special service soldiers first marched 500 miles (805 kilometers) through hot, bug-filled jungles. They then fought thousands of Japanese troops and captured an important airfield.

CONFLICT:
AT A GLANCE

Myitkyina
Campaign

World War II

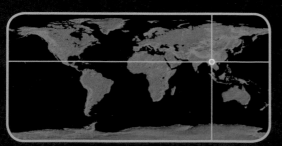

May 17, 1944

Location:
Myitkyina Airfield,
Burma

Mission goal:
capture an
enemy airfield

Mission outcome:
airfield captured

8

1900

2000

Operation
Raincoat

Cabanatuan Operation

January 30, 1945

In 1945 the Alamo Scouts used **guerrilla warfare** to free Allied prisoners. They hiked for miles through rough country in the Philippines. Then they raided an enemy prison at night. The Scouts helped free more than 500 prisoners of war (POWs).

guerrilla warfare—a type of military action using small groups of fighters to carry out surprise attacks against enemy forces

CONFLICT:
AT A GLANCE

Cabanatuan Operation **World War II**

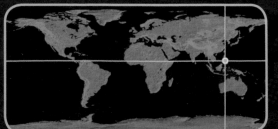

January 30, 1945

Location:
Cabanatuan,
Philippines

Mission goal:
free Allied troops
from enemy prison

Mission outcome:
more than 500
prisoners released

The Alamo Scouts performed more than 80 dangerous missions without losing a single man.

Λ Hundreds of POWs were treated at a hospital after being freed from Cabanatuan prison.

1900

Operation Raincoat

Myitkyina Campaign

2000

Battle of Nam Dong

July 6, 1964

During the Vietnam War (1959–1975), Special Forces soldiers taught the **Montagnard** people combat skills. In 1964 they fought alongside the Special Forces at Camp Nam Dong. Together they defeated the enemy and won the five-hour battle.

Montagnard—local people who live in the highlands in central Vietnam

CONFLICT:
AT A GLANCE

Battle of
Nam Dong

Vietnam War

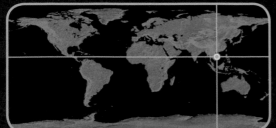

July 6, 1964

Location:
Nam Dong,
Vietnam

Mission goal:
train local people
for battle

Mission outcome:
defeated enemy
forces

Special Forces soldiers trained the Montagnards to carry out ambushes, raids, and other combat skills.

1900

Operation
Raincoat

Myitkyina
Campaign

Cabanatuan
Operation

2000

Fight at Chau Phu

January 31–February 1, 1968

In 1968 two enemy **battalions** attacked Chau Phu, Vietnam. Sergeant Drew Dix led a small group of South Vietnamese soldiers to help defend the city. His small group captured or killed nearly 60 enemy troops. They also helped rescue 14 **civilians**.

battalion—a large unit of soldiers

civilian—a person who is not in the military

Fight at Chau Phu

Vietnam War

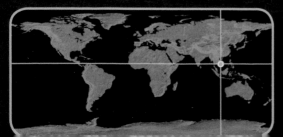

January 31–February 1, 1968

Location: Chau Phu, Vietnam

Mission goal: defend Chau Phu

Mission outcome: defeated enemy forces and rescued civilians

SPECIAL FORCES
ARCHIVES
★ ★ ★ ★ ★

Staff Sergeant Dix was the first Special Forces soldier to be awarded the Medal of Honor. Special Forces soldiers were awarded 17 Medals of Honor during the Vietnam War.

Staff Sergeant Drew Dix (far right) >

Soldiers in Vietnam often fought dangerous battles door-to-door to clear city buildings of enemy troops.

1900   2000

Operation
Raincoat

Myitkyina
Campaign

Cabanatuan
Operation

Battle of
Nam Dong

Operation Just Cause

December 20, 1989 –
January 31, 1990

In 1989 major conflicts broke out in Panama. Many U.S. citizens living there were in danger. The U.S. military invaded the country to remove leader Manuel Noriega. Special Forces teams stopped an enemy **convoy** and captured the airport. Noriega surrendered on January 3, 1990.

convoy—a group of vehicles traveling together, usually accompanied by armed forces

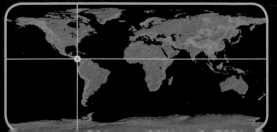

CONFLICT:
AT A GLANCE

Operation Just Cause **Invasion of Panama**

December 20, 1989
– January 31, 1990

Location:
Panama City, Panama

Mission goal:
capture Manuel Noriega

Mission outcome:
Noriega surrendered

SPECIAL FORCES ARCHIVES

★ ★ ★ ★ ★

The **motto** of the U.S. Army Special Forces is "De Oppresso Liber!" or "To free the oppressed!"

∨ U.S. soldiers scouted roads, bridges, and roadblocks near Panama City.

motto—words or a saying that tells what someone believes in or stands for

1900   2000

Operation
Raincoat

Myitkyina
Campaign

Cabanatuan
Operation

Battle of
Nam Dong

Fight at
Chau Phu

Operation Desert Sabre

February 24–28, 1991

Iraqi **dictator** Saddam Hussein invaded Kuwait in 1990. In 1991 U.S. Special Forces sneaked behind enemy lines to gather information on Iraq's army. The information helped U.S. and allied forces defeat Iraq's military in less than 100 hours.

dictator—someone who has complete control of a country, often ruling it unjustly

CONFLICT:
AT A GLANCE

Operation
Desert Sabre

Persian Gulf War

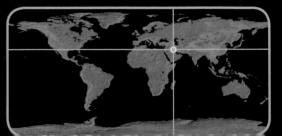

February 24–28, 1991

Location:
Kuwait and Iraq

Mission goal:
gather information
for allies

Mission outcome:
Iraqi forces defeated

SPECIAL FORCES
ARCHIVES
★ ★ ★ ★ ★

During Operation Desert Sabre allied forces destroyed 1,400 armored vehicles and more than 3,000 tanks.

1900

2000

Operation
Raincoat

Myitkyina
Campaign

Cabanatuan
Operation

Battle of
Nam Dong

Fight at
Chau Phu

Operation
Just Cause

Battle of Mazar-e Sharif

October 19–November 10, 2001

In 2001 soldiers in Task Force Dagger were sent to fight **terrorists** in Afghanistan. The soldiers first traveled with local fighters to Mazar-e Sharif. Then they called in air strikes to hit the terrorist stronghold. The soldiers helped capture the city and its important airfields.

terrorist—someone who uses violence and threats to frighten people into obeying

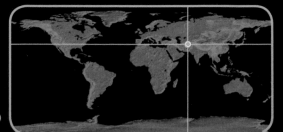

Every Green Beret must learn a foreign language. Soldiers must also study the culture of countries where that language is spoken.

∧ To reach Mazar-e Sharif, Special Forces soldiers rode horses through rough mountain country.

1900   2000

Operation
Raincoat

Cabanatuan
Operation

Myitkyina
Campaign

Battle of
Nam Dong

Operation
Just Cause

Fight at
Chau Phu

Operation
Desert Sabre

Battle at Qala-i-Jangi Fort

November 25–December 1, 2001

In 2001 U.S. forces held hundreds of **Taliban** prisoners at the Qala-i-Jangi Fort in Afghanistan. In November the prisoners **ambushed** the guards and captured many weapons. Task Force Dagger soldiers fought alongside allies to defeat the prisoners.

Taliban—a radical group that controlled much of Afghanistan in the 1990s and early 2001

ambush—to hide and make a surprise attack

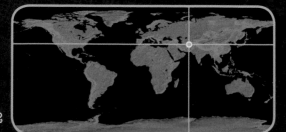

CONFLICT:
AT A GLANCE

Battle at
Qala-i-Jangi Fort

War in Afghanistan

November 25–December 1, 2001

Location:
Qala-i-Jangi Fort
near Mazar-e Sharif,
Afghanistan

Mission goal:
defeat prison uprising

Mission outcome:
all prisoners captured
or killed

▼ U.S. soldiers worked with local fighters to help defeat the prison uprising.

1900

Operation
Raincoat

Myitkyina
Campaign

Cabanatuan
Operation

Battle of
Nam Dong

Fight at
Chau Phu

Operation
Just Cause

Operation
Desert Sabre

2000
Battle of
Mazar-e Sharif

Invasion of Iraq

March 20–May 1, 2003

In 2003 the U.S. military **invaded** Iraq to find terrorists and remove Saddam Hussein from power. Special Forces soldiers worked behind enemy lines to locate enemy positions. They also destroyed enemy missiles and other weapons. The invasion was a huge success.

invade—to send armed forces into another country

Invasion of Iraq

Iraq War

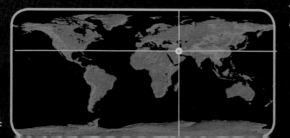

March 20–May 1, 2003

Location:
Iraq

Mission goal:
support invasion
of Iraq

Mission outcome:
invasion successful,
Iraqi government fell

V Hundreds of tanks and armored fighting vehicles were used in the invasion of Iraq.

1900

Operation
Raincoat

Cabanatuan
Operation

Myitkyina
Campaign

Battle of
Nam Dong

Fight at
Chau Phu

Operation
Just Cause

Operation
Desert Sabre

2000

Battle of
Mazar-e Sharif

Battle at
Qala-i-Jangi Fort

Exercise Flintlock

one month each year since 2006

Terrorism is a worldwide threat. Each year since 2006, Special Forces teams go to Africa for one month. They work with soldiers from around the world to fight terrorists. They train soldiers in **sabotage** and other special warfare tactics.

sabotage—to purposely damage or destroy property

CONFLICT:
AT A GLANCE

Exercise Flintlock

War on Terror

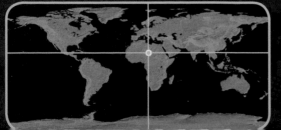

one month each year since 2006

Location: various countries in northern Africa

Mission goal: train soldiers to fight terrorism

Mission outcome: prevention of several terrorist activities

1900

Operation
Raincoat

Myitkyina
Campaign

Cabanatuan
Operation

Battle of
Nam Dong

Operation
Just Cause

2000

Battle of
Mazar-e Sharif

Battle at
Qala-i-Jangi Fort

Invasion
of Iraq

Elite Warriors

U.S. Army Special Forces soldiers have carried out special missions for more than 60 years. They fight in battles. They gather information. They train soldiers from other countries. These elite soldiers work hard to make the world safe.

Glossary

Allies (AL-lyz)—a group of countries united against Germany during World War II, including France, the United States, Canada, Great Britain, and others

ambush (AM-bush)—to hide and make a surprise attack

battalion (buh-TAL-yuhn)—a large unit of soldiers

civilian (si-VIL-yuhn)—a person who is not in the military

convoy (KON-voy)—a group of vehicles traveling together, usually accompanied by armed forces

dictator (DIK-tay-tuhr)—someone who has complete control of a country, often ruling it unjustly

elite (i-LEET)—a group of people who have special advantages or talents

guerrilla warfare (gur-RIL-lah WOR-fair)—a type of military action using small groups of fighters to carry out surprise attacks against enemy forces

invade (in-VADE)—to send armed forces into another country

Montagnard (mon-tuh-NYAHRD)—local people who live in the highlands in central Vietnam

motto (MOTT-oh)—words or a saying that tells what someone believes in or stands for

sabotage (SAB-uh-tahzh)—to purposely damage or destroy property

Taliban (TAL-i-ban)—a radical group that controlled much of Afghanistan in the 1990s and early 2001

terrorist (TER-uhr-ist)—someone who uses violence and threats to frighten people into obeying

unconventional (uhn-kuhn-VEN-shuhn-uhl)—a way of fighting that is not like ordinary hand-to-hand combat

Read More

Besel, Jennifer M. *The Green Berets.* Elite Military Forces. Mankato, Minn.: Capstone Press, 2011.

Bozzo, Linda. *Green Berets.* Serving in the Military. Mankato, Minn.: Amicus High Interest, 2015.

Gordon, Nick. *Army Green Berets.* U.S. Military. Minneapolis: Bellwether Media, 2013.

Newman, Patricia. *Army Special Forces: Elite Operations.* Military Special Ops. Minneapolis: Lerner Publications Company, 2014.

Internet Sites

FactHound offers a safe, fun way to find Internet sites related to this book. All of the sites on FactHound have been researched by our staff.

Here's all you do:

Visit *www.facthound.com*

Type in this code: 9781491487020

 Super-cool stuff!   Check out projects, games and lots more at **www.capstonekids.com**

Critical Thinking Using the Common Core

1. Describe how unconventional warfare tactics help Special Forces teams achieve their missions. (Key Ideas and Details)

2. In your own words, explain why it is important for Special Forces teams to train soldiers from around the world to fight terrorism. (Integration of Knowledge and Ideas)

Index